vs. The Garden

Keeping the Enemy Out!

Billy Thompson

The Field vs. The Garden

ISBN-13: 978-1482796025

Published by
Thompson Intellectual Properties
(DBA B&J Publishing.)

Thanks to:
Timothy & Brenda Judkins
Two people who really love Jesus.

Dear Reader:

Sin is a struggle that we deal with daily. Some have said upon sinning that 'it just happened.' I do not agree. Sin is something that we are either fleeing from or fleeing toward every moment of every day. The Holy Spirit is here to guide us into all righteousness. Those who are led by the Spirit are the sons of God.

The Holy Spirit wants to help us get the upper hand over the sins that entangle us. The writer of Hebrews encourages us to lay aside the weights and the sin that so easily hold us back.

As it relates to our struggle with sin, I have pondered the following three questions: How does sin get into our lives in the first place? Can we get it out? Can we keep it out?

James says, "when we are tempted, we are tempted of our own lust." In other words, outer sins connect with inner desire. We cannot say, "The devil made me do it," though he does influence us. James also tells us that when we submit to God and resist the devil, he will flee from us. In this book, I will expose our real enemy and explain how to keep him out of our lives.

Introduction

My great-grandmother lived alone in the country, and she had a lot of cats. One day as a kid, I asked her why she had so many. She told me that it was to get rid of snakes. I laughed and thought that surely she was joking. "Could there be snakes around here?" Then one night, I went into her bathroom, and lo and behold, there was a big snake in the house. Not only was it in the house, it was curled around the toilet.

I ran out of there fast. It wasn't that I had never seen a snake before. I had, but a snake in the house was too much. I told her that she needed to get some new cats because the old ones weren't doing their job.

God made man and put him in a Garden. The serpent convinced the man and his wife to disobey the direct command of God Almighty. That serpent was a representation of the devil himself.

In this discourse, I would like to reexamine the story of Adam and Eve for the purpose of considering just how the serpent was able to enter into the Garden to begin with.

I don't know how that snake got into the house and past my great-grandmother's cats, but I think I recognize how that serpent got into Adam's Garden.

I believe that if we can establish just how he (the serpent) got into Adam's Garden, then we can prevent him from coming into ours.

Contents

1

Created for Adam

When the Lord God formed man from the dust of the ground, man was merely a hunk of lifeless clay until the day God breathed into man's nostrils the very breath of life.

The Lord God had planted a garden on the east side of the land of Eden. The word 'planted' denotes both time and a process. God simply *spoke* the worlds into existence, but He *formed* man and He *planted* a garden. This shows God's particular care to details.

Everything that God made in the garden was for the benefit and pleasure of His creation. The sun was created for man's warmth and light, the stars for signs and seasons, the herbs and trees were for man's food.

In Psalms 50, God said that if He were hungry, He wouldn't tell mankind. Man has nothing to offer his Creator except for love and devotion. Jesus told the disciples that He had meat (food) that they knew nothing about. And that He Himself was the very Bread of Life by which man should eat and live.

All things that were made on this earth were made with mankind in mind. The very days of the week were made for humanity. One Sabbath, the religious leaders were upset at Jesus for healing a man on the Sabbath. Jesus told the religious leaders that man was not made for Saturday, but Saturday was made for man. Even the days of the week are gifts to man. God does not want us to overwork ourselves. Rest is also one of His gifts.

2

The Significance of East

Notice that the garden was positioned in the East. Solomon built his temple in the East. When the Jews prayed, they would turn to the East in the direction of the Temple. The return of Jesus is likened unto the light; it will come from the East to the West.

The Sun rises in the East. Malachi said that the Sun of righteousness (Jesus) would rise with healing in His wings. The garden was in the East because it represented the place of the light of the glory of God.

In Genesis 11, the earth had only one language, and the people journeyed from the East to the plain of Shinar. They were more than just leaving a physical direction on a map. They were leaving from the East, or spiritually from the place of the revelation of God, and thus going after their own way.

God put the Garden in the East. Eden was the appointed place and east was the appointed direction. Genesis 13:10-11 says that Lot journeyed east because the land appeared to be as the Garden of Eden. He was wrong, for righteousness was not in Sodom. The Bible says that the wise men from the East came looking for Jesus.

One way the enemy comes into our lives is by presenting various alternative ways to God. The Bible says that there is a way that seems right unto a man, but in the end, it leads to death. Jesus said that He is the only way to the Father. Many today believe that all roads lead to Heaven. This is not true. Jesus is the only way.

3

Where is Adam?

When Adam disobeyed, God came down in the cool of the day and inquired of man's whereabouts. This was more of a spiritual issue than a physical one, for God had not misplaced His creation.

Adam was hiding behind the trees, but still in the very Garden where God had placed him. God wanted Adam to acknowledge that he was spiritually out of position. It is possible to be naturally in the place where God wants us, and yet, to be spiritually out of position.

The Pharisees sat in the seat of Moses, but they did not have the same heart as Moses. Satan loves it when we praise God with our lips, but our hearts are far from God. One of Satan's main objectives has been to get us out of God's presence. The Bible says that our sins have separated us from our God. Where is Adam? Where are you? Where am I?

4

Adam's Responsibility

God gave man responsibility in the Garden. He was to dress it and to keep it. First, by dressing it, he had the role of making it look nice. Jesus said that God is the Gardner that prunes the vines. Adam was supposed to care for the Garden. Then he had to keep (protect) the Garden. He was not to allow insects, animals, or anything to spoil the vines. He was to accomplish this task by subduing the earth and exercising God's dominion over it.

He was supposed to represent God on earth. He was to exercise God's authority. He was to exercise the same authority over the earth that God did over the heavens.

God gave man His dominion. This dominion had three levels. They were natural, but they have spiritual significance. Level one was over the fish of the sea; level two was over the fowl of the air; and level three was over everything that creeps on the earth.

This dominion covered everything except other men, for all men were made in the likeness of God. Human enslavement is against nature. It is to put the image of God under subjection to the image of God.

God was so against this that Ezekiel said, "if a beast slaughtered a man that beast must be killed, for he killed one that bore the image of God."

Again, these levels were natural, but they carried spiritual significance. The first level of dominion over the fish of the sea speaks to a dominion over things that are obviously underneath men. There are some challenges that we face that seem menial. We call them "sweat-less victories." They require little effort, just patience.

The second level over the fowl of the air speaks to a dominion over things that seem to be over man's head. Jesus said that if we had faith, we could command the mountains to move from this place to that place, and they would obey us. This level of authority is over the mountains that seem to tower over us. These are the big problems in life.

The last level is over that which creeps on the earth with man. This level of dominion means that man controls that which is equal to him. Some things are a struggle that we deal with on a daily basis. Paul said that there was a thorn in his flesh. It stayed with him daily. These are things that we can conquer; they are on our level. We look these problems in the eye every day.

These three things consisted of minor, major, and day-to-day problems. These things were to be under the dominion of man. The devil wanted man to lose those levels of dominion. Nothing was to dominate man but God. Satan wanted to see this dominion lost. As a mere beast of the field, man had authority over the serpent.

Jesus went about doing good works and healing all who were oppressed by the devil. Satan loves to see people bound. Many people are bound to drugs. This is unfortunate as man once dominated the plants and herbs, but now the plants and herbs are dominating man.

5

A Suitable Helpmate

Adam wasn't moping around the Garden complaining that he was lonely in that big Garden by himself. No. It was God who noticed Adam's plight, and it was the Lord who searched to find a suitable helper for him.

God formed the beasts of the field and the fowls of the air from the same ground. He brought these creatures to Adam to see what he would call them, and Adam gave names to all of them. Of all of the creatures, none was found to be a helpmate that was suitable for him.

God never considered matching Adam with one of the animals. The Bible gives strict prohibitions of intimate human and animal relations.

However, God did allow Adam to see why none of the animals would be suitable for him, lest Adam should come to think that they were. Adam could not carry on an intelligent conversation with any of the animals. He did not have common ground with any of them.

Actually, the ground may have been the only thing that they did have in common. Both Adam and the animals were formed from the same ground. But none of them bore the image of the Almighty. Only man has a spirit.

6

The Garden and the Field

God planted the Garden, and it was there that He put Adam. Adam was not made in the Garden. He was placed there after his creation. Like all the other creatures, he was made from the ground (the field which surrounded the Garden). A river went out of the Garden and split into four parts. It ran through the lands of Havilah, Ethiopia, and Assyria. The Garden was in the midst of these lands. They surrounded the Garden. The Garden was the center of God's creation.

Many animals are native to certain lands. Elephants, for example, are native to Africa, as horses are to Spain. God brought the beasts of the fields from around the world into the Garden to see what Adam would call them.

The beasts were able to come in, but their place was not to stay in the Garden. Their place was in the fields. Again, the Garden was made for man. The air was made for the fowl. The sea was made for the fish, and the field was made for the beasts. None of them were found suitable to stay with Adam in the Garden as his helper. The woman, also, after being taken out of man's side, was brought by God to Adam in the Garden.

"Wilderness" was another term for the field. Moses was leading Israel to the Promised Land, a land flowing with milk and honey. The Promised Land was a type of Garden of Eden, but they first had to go through the wilderness (field) where snakes were. On one occasion, the snakes killed so many people that Moses prayed for help. God told him to build a brazen serpent to bring about the cure.

Jesus was led by the Spirit into the wilderness to be tempted by the devil. It was there that He was alone with the beasts (demons). Beasts symbolically represent demons. After Jesus' temptation, the angels came and ministered unto Him. He was weak from fasting and dealing with demonic powers.

The evil, demonic nations in the book of Revelation are portrayed as beasts. The battle with the devil is always in the wilderness. Israel wandered in the wilderness for forty years. In Revelation, the woman gives birth to the Ruler of the Nations, but Satan is after her. She flees to the wilderness where God prepares a place of protection for her from the enemy who is ready to devour her child.

A war breaks out in the heavens. The devil is cast down to the earth. The war comes to earth. Ezekiel says that Lucifer was in the Garden of God. Heaven was God's garden and Lucifer was cast out of it. Now he is with us.

The Song of Solomon talks a lot about gardens. Solomon warns us to keep the foxes (beasts or demons) out of the garden because they will spoil the vines while the grapes are still tender. Foxes have no business in the garden; they are beasts of the field.

Solomon tells us that, in order to protect a garden, it must first be kept enclosed. Everyone should not be allowed in and out of our garden (life). Solomon's lover gives an invitation for the Beloved to come into her garden. The garden is for the gardener, and those who are invited into it. Everyone else is an intruder. The thief comes to kill, steal, and destroy. Satan has no legal right into our lives unless we give him an invitation. Otherwise, he is a trespasser.

Jesus said that He was the vine and His Father was the Gardener. The garden must be pruned. Anything that does not produce fruit in the garden is to be burned and discarded by the Gardener.

The field is wild. In the field, Jesus said that the wheat and tares would have to grow together until the Father separated them. No one prunes the field. The wild beasts are present there.

An angel was sent to keep the entrance to the Garden of Eden. Angels also stand to protect the twelve gates of Heaven. One doesn't think of Heaven as needing protection, but it does have gates. What is the purpose of a gate? A gate is to keep things in or to keep things out. The angel of the Lord protected Israel in the wilderness, but no angel is ever sent to protect the wilderness itself. During the Tribulation, the saints are told to flee to the wilderness where God will protect them. Notice that God is not protecting the wilderness, but rather, His people.

7

What Happened to the Serpent?

God told the serpent that he would be cursed above all the cattle and every beast of the field. To whom much is given, much is required. The serpent was more subtle or astute than any beast of the field, and therefore, received a greater curse than any other beast of the field. The entire creation came under a curse. Romans says that the whole of creation groans for redemption and the manifestation of the sons of God.

God said that the serpent would have to go on his belly. This could mean that, at one time, the serpent walked into the Garden on legs (or flew). It may have walked into the Garden, but now it would have to crawl out. It would also have to eat dust all the days of its life. Dust is the very substance of which man was made. The serpent was sentenced to the arena of dust (flesh). The serpent's meat became dust (Isaiah 65:25). The serpent had developed an appetite for flesh. It desires to bite dust (or man).

8

What did God Say?

The strangest thing is not that the serpent spoke (for all animals communicate on some level), but that he spoke contrary to the voice of God. God made Adam and Eve in His own image. The serpent told them that they could become like God. In one sense, they were already like God—created in His very image and likeness. The serpent told them that God was trying to keep them from enjoying their lives to the fullest. The reality is that God was really trying to keep them from death.

The serpent was the first drug dealer. He offered an herb that would guarantee mankind a high. "Take it, taste it. It is good for you. It will make you feel good." It was a high; it promised to make them like the most high. But, as with any high, the low that is certain to come afterwards is not worth it.

Most illegal drugs are initially given for free, but the real cost comes later. Eve thought that the fruit was good for food, but she found that the wages of sin was death. The serpent makes things seem good to us that God Himself has declared as not good. Watch out for the voice of the enemy. Jesus said that His sheep would know His voice, and a stranger they would not follow.

When God came into the Garden, Adam and Eve were naked. But they had borne no shame. After partaking of the forbidden fruit, they were shameful. God asked them, "Who told you that you were naked?" They had listened to the wrong voice.

The prophet Balaam was asked one day to curse Israel, but God told Balaam that he was not allowed to curse Israel because He had already blessed them. You cannot call "cursed" what God has already called "blessed".

Peter refused to eat food that he perceived in a vision to be unclean. God told Peter not to call "common" what He called "clean". The enemy will tell us we are too ugly, too fat, too skinny, too dark-skinned, or too light-skinned. But God tells us that we are fearfully and wonderfully made.

We are not to believe every spirit. The Christians in the city of Berea checked the scriptures daily to verify if Paul spoke the truth to them. Jesus told people to search the scriptures, for they testified to the truth. Anything that does not line up with God's word is a lie of the devil. He is a liar and the father of it. If it is contrary to God's Word, then it is the voice of the serpent.

The voice of God came walking in the Garden. God wants us to hear Him, but sometimes, we listen to another voice instead. Is there a serpent in your garden?

Jesus told His disciples that the prince of this world (Satan) was approaching, but that he would not be able to find a trace of himself in Jesus. Jesus was saying that the serpent would not be able to find any of the serpent-like traits in His life (garden). He did not bear the image of the serpent. He was not the seed of the serpent. He was the seed of the woman and the express image of God. Jesus was the Son of Man and the Son of God. He bore the image of man and God, not that of the serpent. As we do a mirror check, whose image do we bear? Is there a serpent in our garden?

9

The Two Adams

In his book to the Corinthians, Paul tells us that Jesus was the second or last Adam. Jesus can be compared to Adam in many ways. Both are called the Son of God. Jesus, of course, was the only begotten Son, and Adam was the first-created son.

There are some differences within their similarities. God took a woman (Eve) out of the First Adam, and He took the Second Adam out of a woman (Mary). Adam ate of a forbidden tree and Jesus died on the tree (the cross). The scripture says, "Cursed is he that hangs on a tree." Adam had to work and till the ground. Jesus worked the works of Him who sent Him.

Adam was tempted by the devil and was thus forced into the wilderness. Jesus was led into the wilderness, and thus, tempted by the devil. Adam, as the head, had to work a cursed ground that brought forth thorns and thistles. Jesus wore a crown of thorns and thistles and bore the curse on His own head.

Adam's wife came out of his side, from a rib. Jesus' bride (the church) comes out of His side from blood and water by the Spirit. Adam's sin caused man to have death, while Jesus' death caused man to be free from sin. Jesus and Adam both had the same enemy—the serpent.

The serpent was told that the seed of the woman would be something his seed would have to contend with. There would have to be a battle. The seed of the serpent would bruise the heel, but the seed of the woman would, in turn, crush the head. This foretold the death and the resurrection of Christ.

10

How did the Second Adam Handle the Serpent?

The first way that Jesus handled the serpent was with the Word of God. The serpent knew the Word of God, but he perverted it. It was Jesus' correct understanding by the Spirit that gave Him power to resist and overcome the serpent. The Word of God is called the "Sword of the Spirit". It is the Spirit who shows us how to use it. It isn't enough to memorize a bunch of scriptures and not know what they are truly saying.

Even the serpent can quote scriptures. It wasn't the true Word of God that the serpent used against Adam and Eve. He questioned them as to what the correct understanding was. He questioned what God meant about not eating of the tree in the middle of the Garden. When the serpent got Eve to see the scriptures through his own eyes instead of God's eyes, he could turn God's own words against His children. Jesus would always correctly quote God's word.

Jesus correctly interpreted many misunderstood passages from the Old Testament in the Sermon on the Mount. He said, "You have heard that it was said... but, I say unto you..." The serpent loves to misquote the Bible.

We need to be careful of people who take scriptures out of their proper context. They are misleading God's people. Jesus said that such people are like their father, the devil.

11

Jesus in the Garden

When Jesus was in the wilderness, He handled the serpent using the Word of God. Jesus, however, did not spend His entire ministry in the wilderness. A great part of His ministry was in a garden. Many times, He would rise early to go and pray in a garden. The Garden of Gethsemane was where He prayed many times. It was there that He prayed for His disciples, His church, and for Himself. Also, it was in a garden tomb that He was buried. After His resurrection, Mary thought that He was the gardener of the tombs, as He appeared to her in another form.

The Bible says that Jesus' disciples knew the Garden of Gethsemane well. At the last supper, Judas was determined to betray Jesus. The Bible says that Satan (the serpent) entered into him. Jesus knew it, and told Judas to go quickly and do what he was determined to do.

After the supper ended, Jesus took His disciples to the Garden of Gethsemane to pray with Him in His final hour. Judas knew the spot, for he had been there with Jesus many times. He led a band of men to take Jesus.

He said that the one whom he would kiss would be the man. Once again, a serpent was in the Garden.

When Judas arrived, Jesus called him "friend". He was not Jesus' true friend. But Jesus knew him well. He was also letting Judas know that the only reason that he was able to betray Jesus in this manner was because Jesus gave him access. Jesus said, on one occasion, that He had chosen all of them, but that one of them was a devil. Jesus knew whom He had chosen.

Just as Adam was betrayed by one of the animals that he had personally called and named, Jesus was also betrayed by one whom he had personally called and named an Apostle. Judas was possessed with the devil (the serpent) himself, and this serpent was able to enter the Garden only because the Son of God allowed him to enter. Jesus said, "No man takes my life, but I lay it down; and I will take it up again." Had the princes of this world known what they were doing, they would not have crucified the Lord of Glory.

Jesus proved that He was in full control of just who could and could not enter in and out of His garden. When they came in with their weapons, Jesus had none. Peter had a sword, but Jesus rebuked Peter for using it. He said that the angels would fight for Him if He needed it. That lets us know that, like in Eden, the angels controlled the entrance into the Garden.

Jesus asked them who they were looking for. They told Him that they were seeking Jesus of Nazareth. He merely said, "I AM," which was the same thing that God the Father told Moses when asked for His name. When He said this, they all fell backwards to the ground. When they finally gained their composure and got up, He asked them again who they were looking for.

At His words, they fell backward, because no one could enter that garden without His permission, including His enemy, Judas.

The question is: why would Jesus allow the devil (Judas) into His garden? It was necessary. Jesus would ultimately bruise the devil's head in the resurrection, but He first had to allow him to bruise His heel by death on the cross.

Our garden is our lives. We can't allow the serpent to make his way into our lives. He is very subtle. He will not come dressed like the devil we see in cartoons. He is an angel of light. He will look beautiful when he comes. He comes in as a handsome man or a beautiful woman. He comes as a temptation. We have to keep our eyes open. God told Cain that sin was lying at the door.

Sin was not yet in Cain's life, but it was waiting. We know that Cain did open the door. Jealousy led Cain to kill Abel. Cain brought unacceptable fruit to the Lord because the seed of the serpent was in his garden (heart).

12

Why was the Tree Forbidden?

God put two trees in the midst of the Garden. They were next to each other. One was the tree of knowledge of good and evil, and the other was the tree of life. Both of these trees belonged to God. God told Adam that he could freely eat from every tree of the Garden—the apple, orange, cherry, fig, banana, etc.. All were meant for eating. But the trees in the midst of the Garden were not for eating but for choice.

Which tree would man choose first? If man ate of the tree of life, he would be partaking of the life of God. Jesus told the multitudes to eat His flesh and drink His blood. They were so offended that many of His disciples left. He told them that He wanted them to partake of His life.

He tried to give the woman at the well, living water. At first, she had no thirst for it. He came to give life and to give it more abundantly. He was the light and the life of men. The tree of life represented Christ.

The other tree was not a bad tree. It wasn't evil at all. Everything that God made He saw that it was good. Even the serpent was the subtlest beast of the field, which the Lord God had made. Lucifer used the serpent, but God created the serpent as good. The tree of knowledge, like the tree of life, was one of God's good trees.

The first tree represented God's life, and the second tree represented God's knowledge. God told man not to touch that tree. It's like a parent telling their child not to go into their room while they are at work. Everything in the room is off limits. The child shares the home, but there are some things that belong only to the owners.

Only God has the ability to know good and evil and still choose good. When God drove Adam and Eve from the Garden, He said, "Behold, the man is become as one of us to know both good and evil." This knowledge is the knowledge of the Godhead; it is too much for man.

It is like the old spy movies where James Bond's mission was to get the intelligence back from the enemies' hands. The C.I.A. is constantly collecting knowledge and is tracking down those who are misusing the knowledge that they have, and thus, threaten the welfare of the world. Knowledge in the wrong hands can be dangerous.

When Moses brought the people to the holy mountain, God told them, "I have set before you life and death, blessings and curses. Now choose life that you and your children may live."

It is a strange thing that God had to tell them what choice to make. Man naturally knows right from wrong. Paul says, "The thing that I would not do, I do." It is a struggle to do right because the knowledge of good and evil can be overwhelming. Jesus was the only man who was tempted and faced good and evil every day, but still chose good every time. Consider when He struggled with His own death. "Let this cup pass from Me," He prayed. "Nevertheless not My will, but Yours be done." He always chose His Father's will.

13

What did Adam and Eve Lose?

They were naked and not ashamed. The word "naked" means uncovered or exposed. Adam and Eve did not have on any natural clothing, but they were covered. They were covered with confidence. They were not ashamed. They were covered with the very glory of God. The glory of God is the presence of God. The Bible says, "For all have sinned and fallen short of the glory of God." David said that man was crowned with God's glory at creation.

The glory was lost at the fall, and the image of God was marred. Jesus told the Pharisees that they were of their father, the devil. The Pharisees were like the seeds of the serpent, for they were doing his works. Satan was a liar and a murderer from the beginning, just as they (the Pharisees) would lie to Him and cause His death. They were acting like the devil.

Humanity now had to make a choice to either serve God, their maker, or serve the self. Mankind lost what it had tried to gain. Jesus said, "What profit would it be that a man should gain the entire world just to lose his own soul?" They lost their souls, but Jesus promised to redeem them.

14

The Little Foxes

The Bible says that it is the little foxes that spoil the vine. Romans tell us to lay aside the weights and the sin that easily causes us to stumble. It is up to us not to allow the little things to bring us down. Sin always starts out small. David's sin did not begin when he slept with Bathsheba and then killed her husband. It started when he should have gone to war as kings did, but instead, he stayed home. David was not defending his garden as he did when he was younger. In his younger days, David killed Goliath to defend Israel, his garden.

Samson's sin was not when he got a haircut. It was when he broke the vow to God to abstain from touching dead things, eating the fruit of the vine, and dating idol-worshipping women.

Moses' anger kept him from the Promised Land. His anger didn't start at the rock, but back in Egypt, when he slew the Egyptian. His anger was never dealt with and became his downfall.

Many people fall into big sins that start so small that no one knows that they are struggling with them—rapists start with lust, murderers start with hate, thieves start with greed.

Jesus taught us how to stay out of sin by putting up a fence around God's law. He said that adultery is a sin, so don't lust. If one deals with lust, he has dealt with adultery. We have to protect our garden from the little things that no one sees, or else, one day, they will be our downfall, and everyone will see it. What is in the dark will come into the light.

When Satan attacked Jesus' hunger, Jesus responded that a man's hunger is to be for the Word of God. He refocused His hunger. When asked if He would bow in worship to receive the kingdoms of the world, Jesus refused because He knew that He was supposed to suffer to obtain them. The Bible says that, for the joy set before Him, Jesus endured the cross. He knew that the kingdoms would become His if He paid the price. The devil tries to satisfy us now. These are the little foxes that spoil the vine—anything that is good *to* us, but is not good *for* us. It is out of God's will, or God's time, for our lives. Keep the serpent out of your garden.

15

Why Doesn't God do Something about that Serpent?

God told the serpent that he would have to crawl on his belly and eat dust all the days of his life. Why dust? Man is made out of dust. The serpent was confined to the realm of dust or the realm of the flesh—and thus, an enmity is put between his seed and the woman's seed.

For this purpose, the Son of God was manifested to destroy the works of the devil. God anointed Jesus of Nazareth with the Holy Ghost and with the power to do good and heal all who were oppressed by the devil. Jesus came to destroy the works of the devil.

When Jesus was here, He could only be at one place at a time. He was limited by His physical body to be in a certain location. He did send His word and heal the centurion's servant. But generally speaking, He could only be in one place at a time.

The Bible says that He called His disciples unto Himself. He told them that He wanted them to go to every town that He would go to and to preach the gospel of the kingdom, cast out the devil, heal the sick, cleanse the lepers, and raise the dead. He gave them the power to cast out devils.

Jesus said that these signs shall follow those who believe; "in my name, they shall cast out devils." Jesus is not worried about the devil.

He beheld Lucifer fall like lightning. When Lucifer became a rebellious angel, a war broke out in heaven. Michael and his angels fought, and the Dragon and his angels fought. And the Bible says that there was no longer any room for them there. Heaven had taken as much as it could stand. The angels began to rejoice, but then they began to mourn for those on the earth, because Lucifer was coming to torment and accuse mankind.

When I first read how Lucifer was cast to the earth, I thought it seemed a little unfair that he should come down here with helpless mankind; but man is not helpless. When God made Adam, He gave him the dominion or absolute power over the earth. His job was to keep or protect the Garden from any and all intruders.

When God brought the beasts into the Garden, it was so that Adam could name them and tell them what they were to be called. Instead, one of the animals decided that he would rename Adam. He called man a god. Adam believed it and submitted to this beast. Through the serpent, Lucifer was able to take Adam's job of naming, and thus, assumed the role of man. Thus, Lucifer became the god of this world.

Jesus was a man, but He was also God. Jesus was God, but He was also a man. This is a great mystery. He shall be called "Emmanuel", meaning God is with us.

Why did God become a man? Why didn't He just declare us saved? He created everything by His words. Surely, He could have just declared us forgiven. Why did it take Jesus' death on the cross?

All analogies are incomplete. Perhaps this one will help a little. Let's say that I gave a friend of mine a new tie for Christmas. I really wanted him to have it.

It is one of a kind and has been made just for him, but he decides to give it away to somebody else.

I go for a walk one day and see a man wearing that tie. I ask him where he got it. He tells me and it is just as I thought—my friend gave him the tie.

Would it be right for me to yank the tie from this stranger's neck and say, "It is mine! I bought it for so and so."? No, of course not. I must go to my friend and tell him that it is up to him to retrieve the gift that was intended for him alone.

When God came down into the Garden, nothing was the way that God had created it. Everything was different. Adam and his wife were now hiding from the very presence of the loving God who made them.

16

Why did Jesus Come?

God is just. God does everything legally. If we sin, we have an advocate with the Father, Jesus Christ the righteous. Satan is called the accuser of the brethren. God will one day judge the world, and the saints will judge angels. The world will become a cosmic courtroom.

When God created the earth, He gave it to man. The earth is the Lord's and the fullness thereof, and yet, Satan has become the god of this world. How can these two statements be true at the same time?

When God gave Adam this world, He gave him absolute dominion over creation, but one creature in creation decided that he would talk. Paul said that he didn't permit women to speak in the church lest she usurp man's authority. This scripture must be understood in its proper cultural context. However, a point can be seen: the serpent was not supposed to speak because, in so doing, he was able to usurp authority over the man. Adam was to speak to the animals and define their character by giving them their names, but the animal is now talking to man and trying to redefine his charter, telling him that he can have more power and even be on God's level.

As Adam and his wife listened to the serpent, they gave the deed of the earth over to Satan. Now he is the god of this world. God didn't give earth to the enemy; Adam did. Since a man lost it, so a man had to get it back. God could not ask Adam to get it back, because man was too weak to stand up to Satan after the fall. Sin put man in bondage.

There were many great men in the Bible, but none were found worthy. David, for example, was a man who followed God. He had a heart to please God, but when he desired to build God a house, he was forbidden because he was a man of war and had blood on his hands. We have to have clean hands and a pure heart to stand before God. Blessed are the pure in heart for they shall see God.

Moses was the most humble of all of God's servants, but his sin of refusing to sanctify God in the sight of Israel caused him to be unable to enter the Promised Land. If time would permit, a huge list could be compiled of all the men who failed in the Bible. That would be every name mentioned. For all have sinned and fallen short of the Glory of God.

So God saw that no man was worthy. John said that he wept, for none was worthy to open the book, but then one of the elders said that the Lamb is worthy. Only God was worthy and sinless to redeem man. Herein lays the mystery of the Trinity.

God was not a man. This was a dilemma. So in the fullness of time, God sent forth His Son born of a woman. Jesus was Emmanuel, God with us. Since there was no sinless man, God put on flesh and became the sinless man.

On the cross, Jesus said, "My God, My God, why have you forsaken me?" For the first time in all eternity, the Trinity was separated.

Even on earth, Jesus would rise early to pray in order to be with His Father. At the age of twelve, He was in the temple going about the Father's business. But for the first time in all eternity, when Jesus was on the cross, sin had separated God from God. It wasn't Jesus' sin. He was sinless. But He took our sins on Himself. The Lord had laid on Him the iniquity of us all.

In that moment, God turned His back not on His Son, but on the sin He became. And, for the first time, Jesus was truly alone. His disciples had fled and His people had rejected Him. But none of that compared to His Father turning His back.

"My God, My God, why have you forsaken me?" God was silent. The earth went into chaos. The sun refused to shine. The earth began to quake. Graves came open and people walked out. What was happening? It was so dramatic that one of the soldiers who crucified Him became convinced that He was surely the Son of God.

Though God was silent, He was speaking. He was saying, "Jesus, man lost it (the Garden) and only man can get it (the Garden) back." He was fully God, but He was also fully man. He died not as God, but as man. It just happened that no man was worthy, so the Word of God became flesh and died as man. Jesus took the keys of death and hell out of the hands of the enemy. Grave, where is your victory; and death, where is your sting? He who lives and believes in Jesus will never die, and he who dies shall live.

17

How Does the Serpent React to Christ?

The serpent was told that the seed of the woman would crush his head. He was on the lookout from that very day. He even sent a fallen race of angelic beings to have relations with the women of earth to corrupt the pure seed of the woman. This sounds strange, but the Bible says that we entertain angels daily unaware. If we can entertain holy angels unaware, then we should not think it strange that we have probably seen both good and bad angels in our lifetimes. The Bible calls Lucifer "an angel of light." He will never appear as a red creature with a huge fork and long tail.

Satan is deceptive. He likes to come in a form that blends in. That is why he came as a serpent. It was one of the beasts of the field. He blended right in. This fallen angelic race was not able to corrupt the entire seed. For Noah was righteous in his generation. Noah found favor in the eyes of the Lord. He taught his sons to be pure. His three sons and their wives had no children. They were protecting the seed. God destroyed the world and spared Noah's family. The seed of the woman was preserved through this righteous family.

When God chose to bless Abraham, Isaac, and Jacob, all of their wives were stuck with barrenness. This was not coincidental. Satan was trying to nullify the seed of the woman before there was one.

In the days before the birth of Moses, there was a rumor that the deliverer was coming. Satan got nervous. He didn't know who it would be, but he influenced the slaughter of all the babies in the land. Moses, however, escaped. In the days before the birth of Christ, there was another rumor of the deliverer, and King Herod killed all the babies in the land. Yet Jesus escaped. Satan tried hard to stop the plan of God, but it didn't work.

Jesus Christ came in the flesh. The Bible tells us that when Jesus first announced that He was the Christ by reading from the book of Isaiah, a devil manifested itself, saying, "We know who you are."

The devils recognized Jesus. They begged Him not to destroy them before their time. The people were amazed that devils were subject to Him.

The devil hates the fact that Jesus came in the flesh. It is one thing to be defeated by God, but another thing altogether to be defeated by God at his weakest state. God, as a man, defeated him. The Bible says, "Here is how we know the spirit of antichrist. Antichrist is any spirit that will not confess that Jesus Christ came in the flesh. He is antichrist that denies the Father and the Son."

This hurts the ego of the serpent. He tried so hard to stop this from happening. Had the princes of this world known what they were doing, they would not have crucified the Lord of Glory.

18

Jesus Protected His Garden

When Lucifer rebelled, there was no longer a place for him. War broke out in heaven, and Jesus saw Lucifer fall like lightning. Jesus didn't allow him to fill heaven with violence. He had Lucifer and his angels cast out and reserved in chains of darkness.

From his youth, Jesus had a love and a zeal for the house of His Father. Heaven was His Father's house. Now that He was on earth, the temple represented His Father's house. At twelve years of age, Jesus could be found sitting in the temple. As an adult, Jesus went into the temple and saw the moneychangers doing business. This angered Jesus. He became filled with a righteous indignation and turned over the tables. Then He drove the moneychangers from the temple because they had made His Father's house a den of thieves.

19

Jesus, Judas, and the Devil

It was noted earlier that both Jesus and Adam had similarities. It may also be noted that Jesus and Judas had similarities. They both died on a tree. Jesus laid down His life by death on the cross, but Judas hung himself on a tree. Jesus went to Paradise, but according to Acts 1:25, Judas went to his own place (hell). Jesus had both a natural and a spiritual son-ship. He was the Son of God and the Son of Man. Judas also had a natural and a spiritual son-ship. He was the son of Simon, and according to John 17:12, he was the son of perdition.

It is interesting to note that Jesus called him the son of perdition. Only one other person in the Bible is given this title and that is the antichrist. According to II Thessalonians 2:3, the man of sin, or the antichrist, is a type of the devil incarnate. Many people throughout the Bible were possessed by demons, but no one is possessed by Satan himself except for two individuals:

the apostle Judas and the coming antichrist. Like Christ, Judas has two natures. According to John 6:70, Jesus calls Judas a devil.

Jesus always spoke to the spirit that was influencing the natural. When a storm came over Galilee one day, water filled the boat. The disciples tried to get the water out. Peter, perhaps, thought that he could handle it. He was a fisherman and had probably been in many storms before. However, when this particular storm became too great, they woke Jesus, who was resting in the back of the boat, undisturbed by a pillow that was nevertheless soaking wet. Jesus rose and He rebuked the wind. It is interesting that the words for "spirit" and "wind" are interchangeable in both Greek and Hebrew. Jesus spoke not to the water, but directly to the wind or the spirit behind the storm. It was the wind that carried the water. The water was not the issue but the wind.

When the Heavenly Father revealed to Peter that Jesus was the Christ, Peter received a blessing for that revelation. However, when he tried to rebuke Jesus, Jesus said, "Get you behind me, Satan, for you say not the things of God, but of men." Jesus was not calling Peter Satan. He was talking directly to Satan, who was now beginning to influence Peter's thinking. Jesus told Peter that "Satan desires to have you that he may sift you as wheat, but I have prayed that your faith holds up."

Just before Judas betrays Jesus, Jesus gives him some bread. The Bible says that afterwards, Satan entered into him (Judas)—not a demon, but Satan himself. Jesus said to Satan, "That which you are about to do, do it quickly."

The difference between Judas and Jesus was that Satan was able to enter Judas, but not Jesus. Jesus said, "The prince of this world is coming, and there is none of him (his ways) in me."

Judas, on the other hand, had some issues. Judas was dealing with greed (Matthew 26:14-15), hypocrisy (John 12:5-6), treachery (Mark 14:43), dishonesty (John12:6), and guilt (Matthew 27:3 & Acts 1:18). These are not characteristics of God but of Satan.

When Mary used expensive ointment on Jesus' feet, Judas' reply was that the ointment could have been sold and the money used for the poor. Judas held the bag of money for the disciples. He was the treasurer. At any moment, he could have helped the poor, but he didn't. He didn't care for the poor; he cared for money. He sold Jesus out for only thirty pieces of silver. Surely, Christ is worth more than any amount of money. Peter and John would one day say, "I do not have silver and gold to give, but I give you Jesus."

We need to make sure that we are not like Judas. He walked alongside Jesus daily, and yet, had so many ungodly things in his life. Satan eventually was allowed to enter Judas' garden. Is there a serpent in your garden?

Paul reminds us that we are not our own, but that we are bought with a price, and that our bodies are the very Temple of the Holy Spirit. Jesus told us that if a house (life) isn't kept clean and swept when a demon is cast out, then he will go find seven more demons that are even more wicked than the first, and then reenter that person's life (garden). The Devil wants to make our bodies his temple, but as Joshua said, "As for me and my house (garden), we will serve the Lord." Is there a serpent in your garden?

20

Protecting their Garden

Jesus went into the home of a man named Jairus, whose twelve-year-old daughter was sick. When he arrived, Jairus had been told by his servants that Jesus would be of no help because his daughter was now dead.

The room was filled with mourners. Jesus made a remark to them that she was not dead but only asleep. They began to laugh at Him and to scorn Him. Jesus had been invited to the home by the owner to heal his little girl. The mourners stopped crying to laugh at Jesus.

So what does Jesus do about it? He puts them all out of the house. It wasn't even Jesus' house, but their laughter was disturbing the atmosphere of faith. Jesus was protecting Jairus' faith. Jesus didn't tolerate a spirit of doubt to come into the garden of Jairus' heart.

When Peter prayed for Dorcas to rise from the dead, he also had to put some people out of the house where she was lying. He had to get rid of those who did not believe in what God could do. Those who talk contrary to God have a different spirit in them. It is the spirit of their father, the devil. Peter put them out, and then he was able to pray her life back into her.

God drove Adam and Eve out of the Garden to protect them. That sounds strange, but it's true. God gave them the choice of the tree of life or tree of the knowledge of good and evil. If they would have eaten the tree of life first, they could have lived forever in their original state of innocence. But since they chose the tree of knowledge first, to partake of the tree of life afterwards would have them living forever in a state of perversion or death.

Man had to be redeemed from the choice of knowledge before they could reenter the place of eternal life. Driving them out of the Garden was for their own good. Parents have to protect their children's gardens. Some television shows, movies, or songs are not appropriate for children. They are filled with the doctrines of devils. Parents have a responsibility to protect their children's garden.

21

How did Paul Handle the Serpent?

It was cold, so Paul gathered some sticks and laid them on the fire, then there came a viper out of the heat and fastened on his hand. The viper was hiding in the sticks. Paul must have picked it up without realizing it, but the heat exposed it.

It hung on to him. He shook it off into the fire and felt no harm. Paul didn't get caught up on the viper; he just shook it off. Those who saw it were anticipating his death. Paul appeared not to give it a second thought.

Paul had just survived a shipwreck. God promised him that he must be brought before Caesar before his death. And, just as everyone expected his death, Paul knew that this snake had no authority to take him out before the appointed time.

When the devil would like to take us out, he has no right. If he had his way, we would have died long before now. But when God has a plan for your life, you don't have to leave until it is accomplished.

Many times, they tried to kill Paul and were not able. But when he was finally killed, he declared that he had run a good race and fought a good fight, and that the time for his departure was at hand. Jesus said that no man could take His life. He would lay it down and pick it up, but no man could take it.

22

How are We to Handle the Serpent?

Adam was to name the serpent and then dismiss him from the Garden. Adam allowed the most subtle beast of the field to live in the Garden with him and his family. We have to be careful that we are not sleeping with the enemy. If we have entertained God's angels unaware, then surely we have entertained Satan's angels of light unaware. Jesus said that the enemy is the one who plants the tares among the wheat. When they start growing together, only the Lord can separate them, but we can watch and pray. And like David of old, we can slay the lion and the bear before he devours our sheep. We must kill Goliath before he destroys Israel. We must protect our garden from the enemy.

Jesus said that those who believe in His name would cast out devils and take up serpents. Some have gotten fanatical and actually tried to handle serpents to prove their spirituality. That is not what Jesus intended. However, Paul was on an island and a serpent bit him. The natives knew that the serpents were dangerous and poisonous. They waited for him to die, but when he didn't, they were amazed. They had seen others die from this same type of serpent. What happened? God was showing these natives that the devil (the serpent) had lost his dominion.

When Paul and Silas were in Philippi, a woman with an evil spirit of divination told the natives that these men were coming with the good news of salvation. Paul could tell that she was under the control of the serpent. He commanded the devil to come out of that woman in the name of Jesus.

Jesus has given us power through His name to put the serpent back into his original place. As a beast of the field, he is subject to a man who walks in God's dominion. Notice that I said, "Who walks in God's dominion." One day, the seven sons of Sceva tried to cast out some devils in the name of the Jesus that Paul preached about. The devils said, "We know Paul and we definitely know Jesus, but who are you?" The devils would not submit to their authority. They did not have any.

God has given His children authority in the name of His Son Jesus, the Second Adam. When Jesus spoke to the wind, it obeyed. When He spoke to curse a fig tree, it died. When He spoke to the deaf, they heard. When He spoke to the blind, they saw. When He spoke to the dead, they arose. He has given us the authority to speak to the serpent with His authority. The serpent will obey the Christ in us. For greater is He who is in you than he who is in the world.

Pray this Prayer: Father in the Name of Jesus I give you my life. I renounce Satan and all of his works. I repent of allowing the enemy to have access to my life. Satan get out of my life. Jesus come into my life. Amen.

Contact Information

Billy Thompson

billycthompson@yahoo.com

Made in the USA
San Bernardino, CA
08 November 2014